Becoming a
SELF
Defined
Woman

Becoming a SELF Defined Woman

By Cindy Stradling

CSP, CPC

Balboa Press books may be ordered through booksellers or by contacting:

Balboa Press
A Division of Hay House
1663 Liberty Drive
Bloomington, IN 47403
www.balboapress.com
1-(877) 407-4847

Because of the dynamic nature of the Internet, any web addresses or links contained in this book may have changed since publication and may no longer be valid. The views expressed in this work are solely those of the author and do not necessarily reflect the views of the publisher, and the publisher hereby disclaims any responsibility for them.

The author of this book does not dispense medical advice or prescribe the use of any technique as a form of treatment for physical, emotional, or medical problems without the advice of a physician, either directly or indirectly. The intent of the author is only to offer information of a general nature to help you in your quest for emotional and spiritual well-being. In the event you use any of the information in this book for yourself, which is your constitutional right, the author and the publisher assume no responsibility for your actions.

Certain stock imagery © Thinkstock.
Any people depicted in stock imagery provided by Thinkstock are models,
and such images are being used for illustrative purposes only.

ISBN: 978-1-4525-4120-4 (e)
ISBN: 978-1-4525-4119-8 (sc)

Printed in the United States of America

Balboa Press rev. date: 11/11/2011

In Appreciation:

To my family and friends for their honest feedback. To Bethel Stoddard for her creative graphics and generous contribution. To Amber Wingfield for her diligence in editing and great ideas

Table of Contents

Meet Bethel

Bethel is the co-creation of author Cindy Stradling and Bethel Stoddard. When Cindy started to work with Bethel, she explained that she wanted a mascot that would represent A SELF Defined Woman. Bethel immediately got to work and started to create various options. After a few conversations, and a lot of diligent hard work our Bethel came to life. It was an exciting creation every step of the way and it was so appropriate to name her Bethel after her creator.

You will become familiar with Bethel as you read the book and visit the website. We are confident you will grow to appreciate and love her as much as we do.

1

Becoming a "SELF" Defined Woman

Introduction

For a few years, I've known that I wanted to write a second book. I had several false starts: I'd sit down and write what I thought I wanted to say, only to get blocked quickly. Then I'd stop and I'd have no idea of what would come next. I knew I could write well about sales techniques and tips. I also knew that this direction was not the one I wanted my second book to take. I wanted to create a more personal experience for my readers.

Despite my relative lack of direction, I stayed with writing, because I knew that when people hear an inner voice telling them to do something specific, they should simply follow that voice. Then one day recently, I had a telephone conversation with my Business/Life coach Lori. She asked how my book was coming along, and I told her that I was stuck. I confessed that I wasn't sure exactly what I felt qualified to write about. I did know, however, that at that moment, what I wanted was to hang up the phone and meditate. I needed to work through the frustration I felt from being unable to move forward with the book project, and to work through the hard time I was having in simply being with myself.

I meditated for a full hour. When I was finished, I brewed a cup of herbal mint tea.

2

As I poured the steaming water into my mug, a thought popped into my head. "Why don't you ask people what they think you should write about?" I instantly regained my energy, and with a rush of excitement I sat down to type a brief e-mail. I sent it to 25 people, requesting that they tell me, in five words or less, qualities they felt I demonstrated that I could share with and teach to others.

Once the e-mail was sent, I glanced through my notebook where I capture my daily thoughts and ideas. I turned to a page on which I'd written, a few months ago, an idea for a sales program. The idea seemed to come to life as I looked at my words. I felt energized and I began to feverishly expound on my idea. That day, within an hour, I created the outline for my new CONNECT sales program along with a draft of a marketing e-mail. I sent this draft to a few sales professionals I knew and asked for feedback on it. They all said I was onto something. I felt relieved—I was on a roll!

Within another few days I'd heard back from most of the people to whom I'd sent the e-mail about my book. I was moved and inspired by the wonderful things people said about me. Their feedback has created the foundation for this book.

During my period of non-writing, I was not achieving integrity with my commitments. When I was "walking my talk," including meditating, exercising, eating well, and listening to others, I was able to write freely.

When I was not honouring these commitments I'd made to myself, I felt stuck in my writing. I see clearly now just how vital it is to honour your word to yourself. This is how the concept of "Becoming a SELF Defined Woman" was born. Through others' comments and encouragement, I realized that I was already living life as my own SELF defined woman. I was living by my own values. So, what does being a SELF defined woman mean to me? It means I…

S = Speak authentically
E = Exude enthusiasm, energy and I am engaging
L = Leverage my strengths
F = Freely chooses my path, responses and actions in life

A "**SELF**" defined woman has a superior commitment to success. She achieves results by demonstrating her power through:

SELF-ESTEEM: respect, worth, high regard, high values

SELF-MOTIVATION: intrinsic vision, driving force, inspiration and action

SELF-EXPRESSION: knowledge of her strengths and core values. She has the ability to be herself and express what is important to her

SELF-LEADERSHIP: commitment. She does what she says she will do, even when she doesn't feel like it. She has self-discipline.

Create for yourself what being a SELF defined woman means to you and live your most powerful life.

Chapter 1

SELF Shaping

We each have our own life experiences. Our experiences do not have to determine the path of our lives. We all get to choose. When I first heard this concept, my initial thought was, "That's easy for you to say. You haven't lived my life." Have you ever said that? Often we get so caught up in the drama of a story or event in our lives that we don't even realize the moment has passed and we can let it go. When we tell our stories over and over—our interpretation of what happened—we keep our upsets, disappointments and anger alive in our lives. I have read this bit of wisdom many, many times by various authors, teachers and mentors, yet I had to encounter it many years before I finally understood it.

Some of my life's events helped mould me into the "SELF" defined woman that I am now. I was born in small town in northern Ontario, and I lived there with my parents and my sisters. When I was four years old, my mother left us. When I was nine, my father married a woman with whom I did not get along well. I was kicked out of school when I was fifteen, and I left home at that time. I moved to Toronto a year later, without a job and just a Grade 8 education. At 17 I got married, and by age 19 I was the mother of two sons. Eight years later I took my boys and left my abusive alcoholic husband. He disappeared one year later, with no contact or support for our sons. Around this time, I returned to school to learn floral design. I used this education to work in different flower shops for the next six years, while I also worked as a waitress part-time.

YES
I
CAN!!!

When I was 31, my sister and I opened a flower shop, but we sold it just a year later because my sister became pregnant with her first child and I couldn't manage the shop on my own. Two years later I returned to school to upgrade my education and learn computer skills.

I began working full-time at a manufacturing company when I was 35. This was the first time in my life that I had no part-time job to supplement my income. For the next seven years I held a variety of positions at two manufacturing companies. My life outside of work changed as well during this time. When I was 40, I quit my smoking habit of 25 years, and I was diagnosed with clinical depression and began taking Zoloft. I married again when I was 42 and I returned to night school when I was 48 to earn a certificate in Adult Education. Two years later I was still working in sales, and I left my second husband and purchased my own condo. At 51 I attended my first 10-day course on Vipassana, a form of silent meditation, which enabled me to stop taking antidepressants. I opened my corporate training company at age 53 and I became a certified coach (CPC) through Erickson College at age 56. Now, at 58, I am writing my second book. I am an author, a speaker, a trainer, a mother, a grandmother, a sister, an aunt and a friend.

I've attended many seminars, workshops and webinars. I've listened to audiobooks and read many more books, all to help my personal development.

In this book, I'll share some of the techniques and disciplines I've learned that have made an impact on my life and helped me achieve permanent change. This book is interactive. Exercises, coaching questions and plenty of blank pages to document your personal journey are included.

I also encourage each of you to send an e-mail to people you know, and ask them for feedback on what you can teach or how you inspire others. Then write your own book as well. So much untapped potential is in each of us, and we can all teach and learn from each other.

My wish is that you develop in the ways that will be the most fulfilling for you. I hope that you use the stories, examples and exercises in this book as a resource and a source of inspiration for creating more of the life you want. Enjoy becoming your own "SELF" defined woman.

In love and gratitude,

Cindy

Notes

Chapter 2

Passion

I used to believe that a person needed to stop wars, save the planet or end world hunger to have a worthwhile purpose. I now know that this is not the case for my life. Though I took a long time to figure out what my life's purpose was, I am clear now that it is to support other women as they work to become the women they want to be. As I do this, I too become more of who I want to be in the world. When I work with purpose, natural passion arises in me, and it is an energy like no other. Even now, as I sit and type these words, I sometimes get so excited about what I want to say next that my fingers can't keep up.

One of my many passions is my business, Athena Training and Consulting. I formed a powerful alliance of some of the top training, coaching and HR consulting talent. Collectively we can address and deliver training on virtually any topic that a corporation could need. I do a lot of cold-calling and business development activities in my daily work. Most people shudder at the thought of having to do this, but if I take too long of a break from contacting clients by telephone, I do not feel as though I am doing an effective job.

I am also a facilitator and coach: I love to lead classes and be a powerful coach for my clients. Through my business, I have the opportunity to provide this for people at all levels of organizations. I am excited to get on the phones so I can bring all our resources to organizations, and ultimately provide continuous learning for people.

Nothing thrills me more than to get feedback from excited participants who are lit up by the new information they have just learned, or when I hear from clients that the people I connected them to were a perfect fit.

Even on the days when I am tired or not at 100% initially, I am again energized and effective once I get on the phones and start connecting with people. Life-long learning is another of my passions. I used to think that I wouldn't amount to much because I only had a Grade 8 education. I know now that this is far from the truth. I have continued to learn and grow in all areas of my life. Years ago I was petrified to stand up in front of a group and speak. The little voice in my head said I had nothing of value to say and people would be bored listening to me. In 1995 I decided to join Toastmasters International after a disastrous presentation I gave to the senior team at an organization

where I worked. I can remember going to a meeting in September of that year and being so intimidated by the speakers that I left and didn't go back until the following February. In hindsight returning was one of the best decisions I ever made. One by one I gave my speeches and gained more and more confidence. I achieved my DTM (Distinguished Toastmaster) which is the highest academic achievement in the Toastmasters program. I then took my learning to the next level and started entering speech competitions.

In 1997 I won first place in the evaluation contest, and in 2002 I placed first in our club's International Speech Content and won again at the Area and Division levels. In 2009 I won the President of Year Award. I am passionate about Toastmasters because I know the skills I learned as a Toastmaster have helped me succeed in life, and that passion pushes me to work even harder at my speaking skills.

I bring a good deal of passion to being a salesperson because I have always believed that it is a great profession. I was delighted when the Canadian Professional Sales Association created their Certified Sales Professional designation. Once I heard about it I started to take their certification programs. I remember the day I went to the CPSA office to complete the final step in their accreditation process, which was an oral exam. I was extremely nervous. My interviewer was a very warm and encouraging woman. She gave me the scenario (which was in an industry where I had no experience) and twenty minutes to prepare a sales presentation. The twenty minutes flew by and before I knew it she was back in the room. I was actually quite pleased at how I handled the objections and flowed through the exam. At the end of the session the interviewer said she was pleased to award me the designation!

I am still very proud of being a CSP and encourage other sales people to obtain their own designations. The process took five years, and it gave me firsthand experience at setting a big goal and achieving it. Very inspiring!

"Passion and purpose go hand in hand. When you discover your purpose, you will normally find it's something you're tremendously passionate about."
Steve Pavli

Notes

Time to Celebrate!!!

(Finish the following statement with what matters most to you)
I am so proud that I: (share a time when you were your passion
for something had you achieve something important in your life)

_____

_____

_____

_____

_____

_____

_____

_____

_____

_____

_____

_____

SELF Defining Questions: PASSION

1)   What am I most passionate about?

_____

_____

_____

_____

2)   How do I experience passion in my body?

_____

_____

_____

_____

3)   What lights me up and energizes me? (When I am doing
this, everything flows and time flies.)

_____

_____

_____

_____

What gets
you out of
bed in the
morning?

When you're
HOT you're
HOT!!!

4)   Where can I bring more passion into my life? What difference would it make if I had more passion?

_____

_____

_____

_____

_____

_____

5)   What is one thing I can start doing differently today to
bring more passion to my everyday activities?

_____

_____

_____

_____

_____

_____

Chapter 3

Persistence

Persistence has served me well as an adult. In fact, I believe my persistence has been the key component in my transition to a successful sales career. During the six and a half years that I worked for florists as a designer and worked my way up to be the store manager. I dreamed of opening my own flower shop. When my sister and I opened our shop, we were elated! Unfortunately, after just one year, we had to sell our shop because of personal circumstances. After the sale, I was hired by a prestigious flower shop to be a store manager.

At first, I thought the position would be great—I knew that I'd have fewer worries than I'd had as a shop owner—but I soon realized that something was missing. Because I was a manager, not a designer, I was unable to use my creativity in creating floral arrangements. I stayed in the position a year and a half, but became increasingly frustrated, so I decided to leave the industry and return to school.

When I turned in my notice to the flower shop, I wasn't sure what educational course I would take, but I knew that staying where I was simply wasn't an option. I worked as a waitress in three different part-time jobs for several months, because I was a single mother to two young boys and I had to make ends meet. After some research, I decided on a program called OIA: Office Information Administration. The program would include courses on software programs, like Lotus 1-2-3, Wordstar, Multi-Mate, and WordPerfect, along with basic accounting. At the time, the program was cutting-edge and would enable me to find one well-paying full-time job instead of cobbling together three part-time jobs. Though nervous, I went to Centennial College to complete an application for the program. All went well until I reached a line asking me how many words

Persistence
"L"
SELF Leadership

per minute I typed. The program's minimum requirement was 40 wpm. I froze. I'd never typed a single word before and had no idea about a keyboard's layout. I was about to give up and leave, but as I walked away something inside prompted me to ask the lady at the administration desk if I could take a typing course. The lady smiled and pulled out a copy of the college's course schedule. Unfortunately, the next course would begin on the same day as the OIA program. Discouraged, I asked if there was any exception to the typing speed requirement. She responded that she didn't think so, but encouraged me to complete the form anyway. So I did.

Not until I'd finished the rest of the application did I see at the top of the page that the prerequisite was Grade 12 or equivalent. I was stunned. Why hadn't I noticed that before? I would never have gotten this far because I'd only completed Grade 8. I simply sat there because I had no idea what to do next. The lady behind the counter noticed that I looked upset and asked me if everything was okay.

I explained to her that I hadn't seen the education prerequisite until just now, and that I only had Grade 8, but I really wanted to take this program. She called me to her desk and explained that I could still take the course, but that I would need to take some supplemental courses first. She outlined the process and gave me the paperwork to complete so I could apply. I quickly filled out the application and returned it to her. She said that someone would be in touch with me in the next few weeks to set up an interview. I left feeling very hopeful and thankful.

As I was driving home that day, I realized that if I rented a typewriter, I could learn to type while taking my supplemental courses. Then I'd be ready to take the test for entrance into the OIA program. I was excited by my plan. Though I knew I would still have to work part-time waitressing, I knew I could succeed.
At a meeting the following week with the administrator of the prerequisites department, she asked me many questions about my financial situation and my goals. When we finished, she said that although I wouldn't receive employment insurance, I could take the program. I left the meeting, feeling the most optimistic I'd felt since my sister and I had sold our flower shop.

On my way home I stopped at the business machine rental place and rented an IBM Selectric typewriter. It came with a typing manual to help me learn the keys. At home I set the typewriter up in the basement, just outside the laundry room. It was a private spot where I could practice without bothering the boys. Every day I went downstairs and practiced.

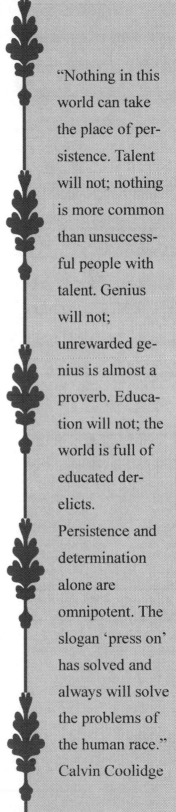

"Nothing in this world can take the place of persistence. Talent will not; nothing is more common than unsuccessful people with talent. Genius will not; unrewarded genius is almost a proverb. Education will not; the world is full of educated derelicts. Persistence and determination alone are omnipotent. The slogan 'press on' has solved and always will solve the problems of the human race." Calvin Coolidge

18

I was frustrated much of the time, as I could never seem to consistently get it right. My mom and sister were excellent typists, so I asked them for advice. Once, when my mom was visiting, I asked her to watch me type to see if she could determine what I was doing wrong. The first thing she noticed was that I was constantly looking at the keys. She said I needed to learn where the keys were: I should only be looking at the book or text I was copying from or at what I had actually typed. She also observed that I didn't really have a typing rhythm, and she suggested I get a metronome to help. I called a local music store and found I could rent one for a couple of months. After several weeks of practice, I set an appointment for the typing test with the college. I wanted to have the test taken so I could go straight into the OIA program when I completed my educational upgrading.

I was very nervous when I sat at the typewriter for my test. My h¬eart was pounding in my chest so hard I was sure Sandy, the lady in the testing center, could hear it. The timer started and I began typing as fast as I could. I looked at the text I was copying and from time to time I caught myself looking at the keys. Before I knew it, the buzzer went off and the test was over. Sandy said she would be in touch with me in a day or so with the results. I wasn't sure how I'd done.

True to her word, Sandy called the next day and informed me I was typing about 18 words per minute. I was very disappointed and asked her if I was able to re-test. She said of course, and just let her know when I was ready.

By this time my other courses had started and I loved my teacher, Eileen Atkinson. She was very warm and inspiring. I had a good deal of difficulty being back in school. Sometimes I would stay up until 2 a.m., working on homework. Looking back, I don't think the work was actually that hard. The real problem was my low self-confidence. I believed that I was dumb when it came to math or accounting. I spent many hours in the library, working through the various exercises we had. I was determined to pass this program.

I also continued to practice my typing and scheduled another test. The test was run exactly like the first and Sandy said she would call me w ith my results. Again I failed, with a rate of only 22 words per minute. I kept practicing and wound up retesting seven more times during the year I took my prerequisite classes. Sandy and I got to know each other well, and she always encouraged me to keep trying. I confess that I was ready to quit school and typing a few times. I was often very tired from working and going to school, and I had very little quality time with my boys during this time.

7 Tips to
Being
Persistent
1. Plan your
work
2. Create &
check
milestones
3. Re-adjust
if needed
4 .Establish
support
structures
5. Celebrate
success
6. Stay
focused
7. Stay
committed

After my seventh attempt at the typing test, I got my usual call from Sandy, only this time her voice was different. I'd passed! To this day, I am not sure if I really did reach the speed of 40 words per minute or if she gave me the mark because of my sheer persistence, but no matter the reason, my persistence and hard work finally paid off.

Returning to school was one of the best decisions I have ever made, and I was absolutely delighted when I was chosen valedictorian for our graduation ceremony. Having a vision of a better life for my family provided me with the determination I needed to get through the two years of being back in school.

Time to Celebrate!!!

Think about a time in your life when you needed persistence to achieve something. Reflect on what values, habits and attitudes were present during this time. How great did you feel when you achieved your goal?

_____

_____

_____

_____

_____

_____

_____

_____

_____

_____

_____

SELF Defining Questions: PERSISTENCE

1)   Have I given up on a vision or dream I once had?

_____

_____

_____

_____

2)   Is this dream still important to me? If not, is there a new vision I would like to create?

_____

_____

_____

_____

3)   If I were to achieve this vision, what difference would it make in my life and the lives of those close to me?

_____

_____

_____

_____

4)	Is this something I would like to commit to? If yes, what do I need to do to get started?

_____

_____

_____

_____

_____

_____

_____

Pleasant

Persistence

Pays

Chapter 4

Compassion

When I was four years old my mother left my father and my two sisters. We were left with our grandmother on my dad's side. I have only a few memories of what life was life when my mom was still with us. When I look at pictures of when I was a little girl, I cannot remember the situations. During my childhood and teenage years I experienced many doubts about myself and my worthiness. I know now that most people have experiences like these while they are growing up, but at the time, I often felt like I really didn't fit in or belong anywhere.

I believe that this is part of the reason I married so young and married someone who treated me very poorly at times. I had very low self-esteem and honestly believed that I wasn't worthy of having anything other than I had in my life. It never occurred to me until much later in life that I, like everyone else, deserve to be treated well.

When I was sixteen I had the opportunity to see my mother for the first time since she left our family. I was nervous and excited at the same time. She came for dinner at the lodge where I was working. I remember how beautiful she was. The first few minutes were awkward but we grew more comfortable with each other as the evening continued. I told her that I was living at the lodge because I really didn't want to go home and live with my stepmother again. She said I could live with her if I moved to Toronto.

After she left I talked to Ericka, the owner of the lodge, and she encouraged me to leave and go to Toronto. I called my mother the next day and told her I would come to Toronto to live with her.

I was excited as we drove into the city for the first time. The time was about 9:00 p.m. and the skyline was absolutely breathtaking, with the lights flickering like diamonds in the distance. When we arrived at her apartment I was a little disappointed, because the only apartments I had seen up to that point in my life were in the movies. Her apartment was nothing like I thought it was going to be. Still, the first few months with her were like heaven. My mom bought me some new clothes, I met all of her friends, and for the first time in my life, I felt special and pretty.

Compassion
"F"
SELF Motivation

This experience didn't last very long, though. My youngest sister Susan called and asked to move to the city with us. My mom said of course and a few days later we went north to pick her up. I was thrilled to have Susan with us. A few days after Susan moved in and registered at school, my mother said I needed to get a job because she could not support all of us. At the time I was hurt that all the attention had shifted to Susan. In hindsight, I know she did the right thing, but at the time I felt almost deserted. There was no discussion or consideration of my future or what I wanted to do. I didn't say anything at the time, and I got a waitressing job.

My relationship with my mother was tenuous for the next thirty years. Most of the time, we didn't see eye to eye. I built up a lot of anger towards her in my early 20s and 30s. We would communicate for a while, but then we'd fight and then sometimes go for years without talking. This always left me feeling abandoned. I started to realize I was carrying anger from my childhood because she left me when I was a baby. In my early 30s, I attended a seminar and became familiar with some self-development books. I began my journey to heal my past. Over the next 20 years I attended many seminars, read many books and continued my spiritual journey. I knew I had a lot of accumulated anger and resentment and I wanted to get past it. One thing that became evident was that I had to forgive her for leaving. When I met new people, I didn't take long to share my sad story with them. Most of the time I got plenty of sympathy and pity. For a while it seemed to pacify me and get me the special attention I wanted.

When was in my early 50s, I was in a program at Landmark Education and doing a paired share exercise. In my usual way I shared my story with one of the other participants named Rita. Her reaction surprised me. She got a very empathetic look on her face and said, "Wow! What must that have been like for your mother, to be 19 years of age and make the decision to leave her three little girls? And then live with that decision every day of her life?" I was stunned. Never once did I ever think of our situation from my mother's perspective. When I got home from the program I called my mom and invited her to dinner.

"Until he extends his circle of compassion to include all living things, man will not himself find peace."
Albert Schweitzer

28

 I could hear she was surprised and hesitant to accept my invitation, but she accepted.

Our conversation was awkward and felt a little strained. I opened a bottle of wine and started to tell her what had happened in the program. I told her that not once in my life had I ever even considered what was going on in her life to cause her to take such a drastic step. I had heard rumours over the years but never bothered to ask her. So that is exactly what I did.

She shared with me what her life was like back then. After she told me about her fearful thoughts and how she was afraid that she would hurt us, she said the only thing she thought she could do was to leave us with someone else, go away and get herself sorted out and come back for us. When we looked back we realized she was probably experiencing postpartum depression symptoms. That evening over dinner, conversation and a bottle of wine, I felt compassion for my mother for the first time in my life.

We have a completely different relationship now. It is not perfect, but we now have tools so we can communicate and keep the relationship moving forward. I think this is the reason a quote by Marcel Proust resonates with me so strongly: "The real voyage of discovery is not in seeking new landscapes, but in having new eyes." By looking at my mother's situation through Rita's eyes, I was able to feel genuine compassion for my mother—and to improve my relationship with her as a result.

Time to Celebrate!!!

When was the last time you experienced compassion for someone? What difference did that make for you?

What acts of kindness can I do today?

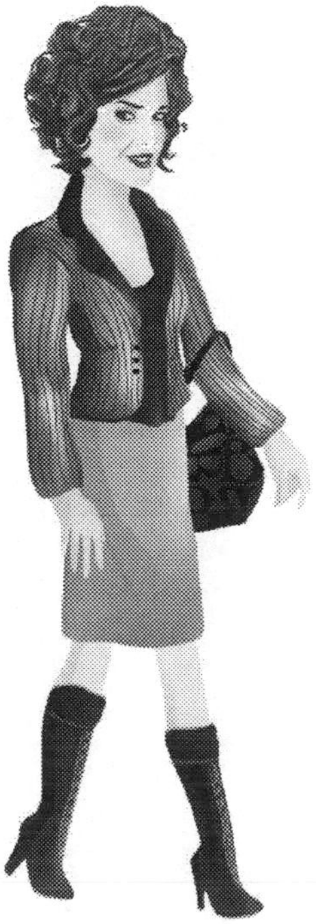

Develop
Empathy for
Others

SELF Defining Questions: COMPASSION

1)   What does compassion mean to me?

_____

_____

_____

_____

2)   How have others shown me compassion? What difference did this make?

_____

_____

_____

3)   How have I shown compassion to others? What difference did this make?

_____

_____

_____

4)   Where is it difficult for me to show compassion? Would having a breakthrough, in having compassion in an area that is difficult for me, provide something different in my life?

_____

_____

_____

_____

_____

_____

5)   Is having more compassion in my life an area that is important to me? If yes, what could I start doing differently today?

_____

_____

_____

_____

_____

_____

Benefits to developing more Compassion:

Scientific studies suggest there are physical benefits to practicing compassion. People who practice it produce 100 percent more DHEA, which is a hormone that counteracts the aging process, and 23 percent less cortisol — the "stress hormone."

Chapter 5

Humour

A good sense of humour is an essential tool for effectively handling life's ups and downs. Years ago I heard a saying that has stuck with me: "Don't take life too seriously; you're never getting out alive." My friends say I have a great sense of humour, and I agree. Though I've had experiences and been through periods in my life that were quite serious, I tend to look at life's lighter side.

Once I divorced my first husband, I took a job as a waitress because I had to support myself and my two children while I attended school to study floral design. As a server at an upscale steak and seafood restaurant, I had to stay on top of everything going on around me. Our restaurant had a well-earned reputation for excellent food and service, and our boss repeatedly reminded us that "the customer is always right."

Around 4:30 one afternoon, an impeccably dressed gentleman rushed into the restaurant. He informed the startled hostess that he was in a hurry and wanted service right away. She placed him in my section of the dining room, and I immediately, brought him a glass of water and a menu. Just as quickly, he ordered a glass of Chablis, the salad bar, a bowl of clam chowder, and grilled red snapper. I steered him to the salad bar so that I could place his order with the kitchen and prepare his wine.

Definition of Compassion (source Dictionary.com)

A feeling of deep sympathy and sorrow for another who is stricken by misfortune, accompanied by a strong desire to alleviate the suffering.

Though I took no more than five minutes to bring him his wine and soup, he was unhappy. He looked clearly agitated, then glanced at his watch and snapped, "You know I'm in a hurry, right?" I told him yes, and I headed to the kitchen to put a rush on his meal. Less than five minutes later, he summoned me to his table. As I picked up his empty soup bowl and salad plate, he demanded to know how much longer the preparation of his fish would take. I responded that I'd check, and I dashed back to the kitchen. When I asked the cook, he barked, "This isn't a fast food restaurant! Good food takes time to cook!"

Back to the dining room I went. When I glanced over at the customer's table. he started back at me, frantically waving at his watch. I had no idea what to say, though I knew I should keep the situation light while easing some of his tension. I reached his table and looked him directly in the eyes.

Humour "S" SELF Expression

"Sir," I said, "you can have your dinner fast, or you can have it cooked. The choice is yours."

He was silent for a few seconds, and then he smiled. "I prefer it cooked, thank you."

The mood at his table instantly lightened. Within ten minutes his snapper was ready. He left me a generous tip, and on his way out he told the hostess that my sense of humour really helped him calm down.

Humour combined with honesty can also defuse situations. A few years ago, my girlfriend Lea and I were going to another friend's place, in the west end of the city, one rainy and foggy October evening. We had never been to Diane's, so once I got off the highway I knew I needed to pay attention to the street names. I hadn't written down directions but I did have a general idea of where her townhouse was. I remembered the name of the street was Buttonville Court.

I was travelling in the right lane behind a bus. As we approached an intersection I could see, above the bus, a street sign that appeared to start with the letter B. Confident this was the street, I signalled right and pulled into the right turn lane. When I pulled over and got a better look at the sign, I realized it said Battleford, not Buttonville. I promptly signalled and pulled back in to the lane I had just left.

This all happened in a matter of seconds and the light had not changed back to green yet. A van pulled up beside me, urgently beeping his horn. Lea and I thought something was wrong so she rolled down the window.

The guy driving the van was cursing at us. He asked me, "Lady, do you know what the &$#?!* you are doing?"

I looked at him and calmly said, "No." He was completely discombobulated.

"A person without a sense of humour is like a wagon without springs. It's jolted by every pebble on the road."
Henry Ward Beecher

Notes

We imagine he was ready for a fight, for us to retaliate, and when we didn't he had no idea what to say next. The light changed to green and we drove off, laughing at the look on the fellow's face. Being calm and keeping your sense of humour in stressful situations can certainly pay off!

Time to Celebrate!!!

What are some of your funniest memories?

_____

_____

_____

_____

_____

_____

_____

_____

_____

_____

_____

_____

_____

Top 10 Benefits of Laughter

1. Relieves stress
2. Lowers blood pressure
3. Boosts self-confidence
4. Relieves anxiety & depression
5. Increased endorphins
6. Boosts immune system
7. Improves alertness
8. Improves heart rate
9. Helps enhance ability to connect
10. Increased energy

Ha Ha Ha !!!

It feels GREAT
to laugh!!!

SELF Defining Questions: HUMOUR

1)   How often do I laugh in a week? Do I tend to see things on the lighter side?

_____

_____

_____

_____

2)   On a scale from 1 to 10, how funny do I find thing? If the number is less than a 7, what can I do to bring more humour into my life?

_____

_____

_____

_____

3)   Who do I laugh with the most? How can I spend more time with this person?

_____

_____

_____

4)   Am I able to laugh at myself?

_____

_____

_____

_____

_____

_____

5)   What difference would it make for me if I had more humour in my daily activities?

_____

_____

_____

_____

_____

_____

_____

_____

Laughter
is the best
medicine!

40

Chapter 6

Faith

"I'll do whatever it takes." I'm sure you've heard that before. In June 2007, I said that when I reached a turning point in my newly formed training and development business. I had been in business about a year and a half and had met with many of the challenges that most entrepreneurs face: near bankruptcy and emotional and physical exhaustion. I didn't know where to turn.

I called my sister Susan and told her I was ready to quit. Susan said, "I guess this is where ordinary people give up." Ouch! Those words stung! Me, ordinary? I didn't think so! At that moment I said, "I'll do whatever it takes to grow my business."

I couldn't know then, of course, that "whatever it takes" wasn't exactly what I had in mind. I began exploring part-time opportunities to give me the cash flow I needed while I continued working 45 to 50 hours a week cold calling, researching, attending client meetings and running workshops. I also never would have thought that "whatever it takes" would include working as a parking attendant during the summer months and being a shoe shine girl for over a year.

Though we've all heard the maxim "give it all you've got," we can't truly understand it until we experience it.

My days as a shoe shiner gave me some powerful insights that I transferred to my business, and have transformed it as a result. Three particular lessons from that period have profoundly impacted not only my business, though—they've also affected who I am.

The first lesson I learned was that "it's not **what** you are doing; it's **how** you are doing it." I'd heard it many times before but not until I was standing at the feet of my first customer, hands on his

Faith
"L"
SELF Leadership

shoes, looking up at a very successful businessman, did I realize that to be successful in this role I needed to change my inner dialogue about who I was and what I was doing. The truth was that I wanted to run away, my stomach was in a knot and I didn't want to shine shoes. Then I reminded myself of my commitment, and I did it anyway. I smiled, chatted and shined. I made a conscious choice to be the best shoe shine girl I could be and it changed the way I shined shoes and interacted with my customers. What was most surprising to me, though, was how good I started to feel about doing "whatever it took," knowing that my commitment was more powerful than my ego or my fears that people would look down on me because I was only a shoe shine girl. I was taking care of business! Suddenly I was proud of who I was and thankful that I got to shine shoes.

This lesson didn't stop at the shoe shine chair. I noticed that it didn't matter what came up in my business's day-to-day interactions; I did whatever it took. If you change the way you look at things, the things you look at change.

The second lesson I learned was the importance of personal excellence and attention to detail. Our customers' appearances were impeccable. They dressed in tailored suits and ties, all coordinated, and by most people's standards they would be considered consummate professionals. Their appearance communicated uncompromising quality. Polished shoes say something important about a person.

They show that details matter, and this attention to detail was so obvious in my customers that I found myself paying more attention to how I dressed and groomed myself. I also concentrated more in my correspondence, communication and proposals because I realized that everything and everyone counts. The experience raised my own bar of excellence.

The third lesson I learned was the importance of consistency. When shining shoes, there is a process to follow: first cleaning, then conditioning, then polishing and buffing to a mirror-like shine. When the process is followed, results are consistent. This seems simple enough, but I noticed that occasionally in my business processes I skipped a step here or there, which yielded inconsistent results.

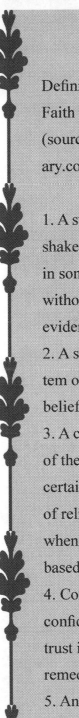

Definition of Faith (source Dictionary.com)

1. A strong or unshakeable belief in something, esp without proof or evidence
2. A specific system of religious beliefs:.
3. A conviction of the truth of certain doctrines of religion, esp when this is not based on reason
4. Complete confidence or trust in a person, remedy, etc
5. Any set of firmly held principles or beliefs

Notes

I didn't think the skipped steps were big deals at the time, but as soon as I paid more attention and followed my processes consistently, guess what? You got it: more consistent results.

When shining shoes, the last step is buffing. In this step, extra depth to the shine can be added, so when customers step down and walk away they have a bounce in their step and they are confident that they look their best. This is also a critical step in our professional and personal lives. In the book <u>212: The Extra Degree,</u> authors Sam Parker and Mac Anderson state that at 211 degrees, water is hot, and at 212 degrees, it boils. With boiling water comes steam, and steam can power a locomotive. I realized that the extra buff, the extra steam, was now showing up in everything I was doing. I had a renewed energy that started to build momentum, which drastically changed my results. My business was growing consistently. Not bad for a shoe shine girl!

Time to Celebrate!!!

When was a time in your life that your faith is what kept you going?

_____

_____

_____

_____

_____

_____

_____

_____

_____

_____

_____

_____

_____

Notes

Notes

SELF Defining Questions: FAITH

1)   Where in my life would changing the way I do things would make a difference?

_____

_____

_____

_____

2)   What difference would it make to add consistency and impeccability to what I am doing?

_____

_____

_____

_____

3)   Are there any areas where I skip a step or two?

_____

_____

_____

_____

4)   If I had 100% faith in my ability to achieve a goal, what would that goal be? What has stopped me from already achieving it?

_____

_____

_____

_____

_____

_____

5)   What are my beliefs about my capabilities? When is my faith the strongest?

_____

_____

_____

_____

_____

_____

_____

Simply start...
Do something today...

48

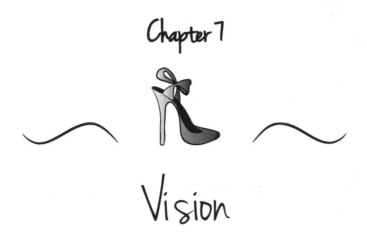

Chapter 7

Vision

In 2003 I'd been using, for five years, a system that I created to help me stay on track and achieve more of the goals I set for myself. This system came about after I had been unsuccessful at reaching the goals I had set as New Year's resolutions for the third year in a row. I was frustrated because I used the SMART goal setting system and I didn't understand what I did wrong. I started to research and experiment with different tools to help me stay on track. I realized very quickly why the SMART system was not enough. Although my goals were specific, measurable, achievable, realistic and had a timeframe, some key elements were missing.

I created a form, which I later called my TICS© chart. TICS stands for "Tenacity, Integrity, Commitment and Structure." These elements had been missing from my previous model. Over time I was able to complete tasks and reach goals that in the past would have simply disappeared. I shared with others what a difference the TICS chart made in my personal accountability. A good friend asked for a copy, which I was delighted to give her. She made a few personal modifications and she too started to achieve more of her goals.

One day when we were enjoying lunch together, she suggested I write a book and share my process with others. I told her that writing a book and creating a workshop were part of my five-year plan.

Although I had never written a book before, I knew I could do it if I used my tool. I was inspired!

I decided to complete a trial, with 10 people using my TICS© chart for a period of three months and documenting the results. After I started tracking what was working and what was not working for them, I created the TENACIOUS goal setting model.

Vision
"F"
SELF Motivation

Change is more difficult that most people realize. To change, we must step outside of our comfort zone, which can result in discomfort.

I've learned through research and personal experience that, after we step out of the comfort zone, we feel a strong pull to return to our old status quo. When this feeling persists, many people give up on the changes they were trying to make. A system to support people through the initial stages of forming new habits until those habits become automatic could result in greater success.

TENACIOUS is an acronym that is designed to provide you with the system from which to set your goals, and the TICS© system is the structure you can use to support you daily to do the activities it takes to make the changes you want.

T – time-bound: Your goal must have a start and stop time.

E – energizing: Your goal must be something you are excited about, and you must understand the benefits of achieving the goal.

N – noted and measured: Your goal must be written and you must have milestones to check for progress, so that you'll know if you're on track

A – achievable: Your goal must be realistic.

C – committed: Your goal must be a personal commitment. Creating an affirmation to support your commitment, especially an affirmation that begins with the phrase "I am," makes achieving your goal more likely.

I – intention and integrity: Your goal must allow you to retain your integrity.

O – opportunity for growth: Your goal must help your personal growth in some way.

U – unstoppable attitude: Your attitude must be unstoppable. When you pause, you must get back on track. Recognize what has stopped you in the past, and then find the structure that will help you get and stay on track this time.

S- specific: Your goal must be specific. Instead of saying you want to lose weight, say that you want to lose ten pounds. Instead of saying that you want to save money, say that you want to save $5000.

Live with
VISION!!!

Have a clear vi-
sion for the fu-
ture and ensure
it aligns with
your most im-
portant values.

The TENACIOUS system works because it gives you a specific place to start. Often, deciding to make a change is the easy part. Frequently we have no idea how to achieve that change or what steps to take to get there. The __start__ of a self-improvement project is what __stops__ most people. A written plan with steps to achieving goals increases the likelihood of success.

In his book "What They Don't Teach You in the Harvard Business School," Mark McCormack tells a study conducted on students in the 1979 Harvard MBA program. In that year, the students were asked, **"Have you set clear, written goals for your future and made plans to accomplish them?"** Only three percent of the graduates had written goals and plans; 13 percent had goals, but they were not in writing; and a whopping 84 percent had no specific goals at all.

Ten years later, the members of the class were interviewed again, and the findings, while somewhat predictable, were nonetheless astonishing. **The 13 percent of the class who had goals were earning, on average, twice as much as the 84 percent who had no goals at all.** And what about the three percent who had clear, written goals? They were earning, on average, **ten times as much as the other 97 percent put together.**

Clearly, goal setting is powerful.

After I created the TENACIOUS system and shared it with ten people, I planned to write about each individual's experience.

Then I changed my mind and instead created a story that included all the events of the ten people participating in my study. I was very excited as everyone started to report positive changes from using my chart.

Next, I created a writing plan that included all the steps I needed to publish my book. I decided on self-publishing since I wanted to use the book to support my workshop.

Through somctimcs I got a bit off track, I followed my plan diligently and got back to work quickly. I used my TICS© chart to schedule and track all my activities. My ultimate goal was to send my manuscript to the publisher on December 31, 2003, and I did just that! The pride I felt as I placed the stamp on the package was so strong. My manuscript for <u>Crossing the Finish Line</u> was completed and on its way to becoming, with me a published author.

Today I still use my TICS© chart in a modified form, along with my BlackBerry, to set and track all of my goals. The specific method you use doesn't matter as long it works for you. My current goal is to continue to write and to become a keynote speaker, sharing how women from all walks of life can choose to become their own SELF defined woman.

Develop your personal Vision statement...

Notes

Time to Celebrate!!!

Write about a time when you had a vision and you took all the necessary steps to make it a reality. How did you feel?

_____

_____

_____

_____

_____

_____

_____

_____

_____

_____

_____

_____

SELF Defining Questions: VISION

1)   Do I have a vision for your life? (This could be in the areas of your career, relationships, retirement, finances, health, family, or anything of importance to me.)

_____

_____

_____

_____

_____

2)   Pick three areas and create a one-year vision and a five-year vision. What do I want my life to be like in one year and five years? Why is this important to me? What is one thing I can start doing today that will help me realize my vision?

_____

_____

_____

_____

_____

Notes

3)   When my vision is a reality, how will this affect my life and the lives of those around me? Why is this important?

_____

_____

_____

_____

_____

4)   What structures do I need to put into place to make sure I stay on track and reach the milestones along the way?

_____

_____

_____

_____

_____

_____

_____

Chapter 8

Generosity

Volunteering is one way that I practice generosity. I've volunteered many times as an adult: I've been a Big Sister, and I've worked with the Salvation Army, the Children's Aid Society, Free the Children, Children's Wish, Leisureworld (working with seniors) and Thornhill Hospice, among my many experiences. Every volunteer position has given me immense satisfaction and I've had numerous rewarding, funny, and inspirational moments. One stands out among them all.

I used to give therapeutic touch and Reiki treatments, and I was approached by my teacher who asked if I would provide weekly healing sessions to a lady who had ALS. Amyotrophic Lateral Sclerosis is also known as Lou Gehrig's disease. ALS is a fatal neurodegenerative disease. People with the disease become progressively paralyzed due to degeneration of the upper and lower motor neurons in the brain and spinal cord. Eighty percent of people with ALS die within two to five years of diagnosis, unable to breathe or swallow.

At that time, I knew very little about the disease other than it was fatal and that the body slowly loses all function while the mind remains active. I agreed to the sessions immediately and was connected with the patient's husband, David. Since I'd already had a police check and medical exam for the other volunteer work I had been doing, there was no wait time for approvals.

At my first meeting with Carol, her eyes said everything. I'd always understood that we communicate in non-verbal ways, and in particular with our eyes. Meeting Carol and being able to receive communication via her eyes only was one of the most rewarding and enriching experiences of my life. She loved our sessions, and I knew she did because her eyes sparkled each time. I was told that her morphine requirement was reduced after each session.

Generosity
"E"
SELF Esteem

David loved her very much and took excellent care of her. He wanted her to have some quality of life and to not just lay there drugged, not knowing what was going on. This meant a great deal of extra support and work on his part. Every time I visited, Carol was immaculately clean and I could tell that, despite her tremendous pain, she appreciated the love and support she received.

At Christmas I gave her a pair of earrings in the shape of trees with flashing lights. Her eyes danced with delight as she watched them flash on and off. I was about to leave, but her childlike mischievous look seemed to tell me not to go. David joined us upstairs and showed me a little computer-like screen where she had, with her husband's help, typed the message "Merry Christmas, Cindy." He explained that, with a contraption that he created, she actually typed the message via an adapter on her ear. I couldn't help crying. She was delighted that she was able to create this for me.

I felt a deep connection to her humanity and I was honoured for the opportunity to be part of this woman's life.

One day as I held her hand, I commented that her skin was so soft. David took her other hand in his and said, "She always took such great care of herself." I could see in their looks that their love was still very much alive. He had such a deep love and respect for her. I jokingly asked if he had any single brothers like him. I sensed she understood my humour when her eyes smiled in approval.

Upon my arrival one Thursday afternoon, I knew something was wrong by the look on her husband's face when he answered the door. He said she was in her last hours and would not need any more treatments. I asked to say goodbye to her, and I was able to kiss her forehead and thank her for allowing me to be with her during the past year. When I got back in my car, I sat for a few minutes in prayer.

Carol died that afternoon. I met her two children at the funeral and they thanked me for my generosity in giving my time to be with their mother. I assured them that the pleasure was all mine and that they were very generous to let me contribute.
I often say we don't have a crystal ball and we don't know what will happen tomorrow, which is why it is so important to live each day and do whatever you can to make a difference. Volunteering is one way we can all be generous.

Give what
you want to
receive

Reflection: Look back on your own life and remember times where you volunteered in any capacity. Think of how you made a difference for others. Write your own story. If you have not volunteered before, consider where you might like to start.

Time to Celebrate!!!

Write about all the times you have been generous in your life.
Use a separate page if needed.

Give what you want to re-ceive...

_____

_____

_____

_____

_____

_____

_____

_____

_____

_____

_____

_____

_____

_____

Definition of Generosity (source Dictionary.com)

1. Willingness and liberality in giving away one's money, time, etc; magnanimity

2. Freedom from pettiness in character and mind

3. A generous act

4. Abundance; plenty

SELF Defining Questions: GENEROSITY

1)   What was most important for me when I volunteered?

_____

_____

_____

_____

2)   How can I acknowledge my generous contribution? (To put it another way, how can I celebrate my success?)

_____

_____

_____

_____

3)   If I have not volunteered before, what areas would I consider if I were to volunteer?

_____

_____

_____

_____

_____

4)   What difference could I make if I either started to volunteer or volunteered more?

_____

_____

_____

_____

_____

_____

5)   Where in my life am I stingy? What do I need to do to be more generous?

_____

_____

_____

_____

_____

_____

_____

Give without expecting anything in return

Chapter 9

Integrity

Integrity is a value that I strive to have in all that I do. In the past, sometimes I've let myself off the hook when I've said I'd do something. Through research and my own experience, I've learned that doing this undermines your self-esteem. Working to cultivate integrity has been prominent in my battle against depression, which I was diagnosed with in 1993. Many times over the next ten years I tried to get off Zoloft unsuccessfully. But every time I tried, I would spiral into a deep depression, become immobilized, and want to give up on everything. My doctor told me to accept that I would have depression for the rest of my life.

One day, at a health fair at my church, I met a naturopath offering a free diagnostic. I filled out the questionnaire and waited for my turn to speak with him. As the doctor read through the information on my questionnaire, he stopped, looked me straight in the eyes and said, "You have to get off those antidepressants. They're killing your liver." I was a little stunned at his directness, but at the same time I paid attention. I told him that I'd tried several times with no luck. I asked if he had any suggestions, and he said meditation had proven to help patients who suffer from depression. I left the session determined to get off the pills forever.

I started my search for a meditation practice. I tried classes, tapes, and CDs, but nothing seemed to work to calm my overactive mind.

A friend told me about a very powerful silent meditation course, 10 days long, named Vipassana. She said she thought it had the kind of rigor I was seeking. At first I laughed because I'm a chatterbox, so the idea of me not talking for 10 days seemed impossible. I researched the program and was very intrigued by the process and the discipline. After much deliberation I went online and signed up. I knew this would not only test my integrity, but that it would also test my tenacious nature. The program was very rigorous indeed, with waking at 4:00 am and meditating, on average, 10 hours a day. Here is an overview of the technique (taken from the Ontario Vipassana website: http://www.torana.dhamma.org):

Integrity
"S"
SELF Expression

"The course requires hard, serious work. There are three steps to the training. The first step is, for the period of the course, to abstain from killing, stealing, sexual activity, speaking falsely, and intoxicants. This simple code of moral conduct serves to calm the mind. . . .

The next step is to develop some mastery over the mind by learning to fix one's attention on the natural reality of the ever changing flow of breath as it enters and leaves the nostrils. . . .during the course is shared with all beings. . . .

67

Finally, on the last full day participants learn the meditation of loving kindness or goodwill towards all, in which the purity developed during the course is shared with all beings. . . .

[The program] is not taught commercially, but instead is offered freely. No person involved in its teaching receives any material remuneration.. . .

There are no charges for the courses - not even to cover the cost of food and accommodation. All expenses are met by donations from people who, having completed a course and experienced the benefits of Vipassana, wish to give others the opportunity to benefit from it also. Of course the results come gradually through continued practice. . . .

The more the technique is practiced, the greater the freedom from misery, and the closer the approach to the ultimate goal of full liberation."

The first three days were very challenging for me. I wanted to run away. My little voice was going crazy, my body ached from sitting and I didn't think I could do it any longer. I kept following my breath as I was instructed and reminding myself of the commitment I made that I would complete the program. All kinds of crazy things came into my mind: things from the past, things that I feared, and things I was anticipating. I understood at an experiential level how out of control my mind could be.

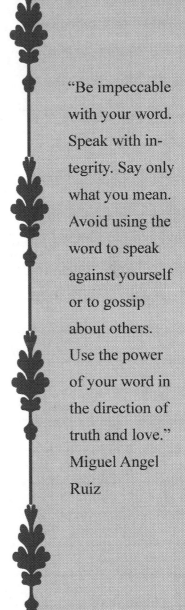

"Be impeccable with your word. Speak with integrity. Say only what you mean. Avoid using the word to speak against yourself or to gossip about others. Use the power of your word in the direction of truth and love."
Miguel Angel Ruiz

I experienced every emotion possible—tears, sadness, joy and everything in between, all in silence.

The program used a combination of audio tapes and video discourses. As I followed the instruction of the teacher, S.N. Goenka, I began to notice how transient my feelings and thoughts were. One minute I thinking about a sales call I had done, the next about an argument I had twenty years ago, and then minute later I was wondering what was going to be for lunch. I could see what Goenka meant by "monkey mind." The impermanency of thoughts was becoming clearer to me: if left alone, they will simply pass. I think I knew this intellectually, but now I knew it through experience.

By day six my mind was quieter, and while the program was still extremely challenging, I was excited to finish the course and get the results. When day ten arrived I actually didn't want to talk initially because I was so peaceful inside that I didn't want anything to disturb it.

When I returned home, I felt an inner joy that I had never experienced before. My focus was incredible and drama seemed to disappear from my life. Though meditating two hours a day upon returning home is recommended, I promised myself that I would meditate one hour per day during the week and participate in one 10-day program every year.

About two weeks after, as I drove on the highway, I knew it was time to get off my antidepressant. The doctor did not agree with me, but I told him I was doing it with or without his help. I explained the Vipassana practice, its benefits and my commitment to daily meditation practice. Reluctantly, he agreed to support my decision, and over the next three months he slowly weaned me off the medication. To this day I have never taken another antidepressant, and I never will.

Does this mean I never get depressed? No, of course not; I do feel down from time to time. The difference is that I now have a healthy way to deal with the feelings.

On most days, I am up at 5:00 am and meditate until 6:00 am. I have attended a 10-day program every summer since. When I come back to the hustle and bustle of everyday living, my mind becomes less calm over time. However, it is still 100% calmer than before I began meditation, and when I have a particular challenge, I often meditate on it.

By continuing my meditation practice, I am able to keep my promise to stay off antidepressants and to face my depression when it arises.

"Always be yourself, express yourself, have faith in yourself, do not go out and look for a successful personality and duplicate it."
Bruce Lee

Time to Celebrate!!!

Share a time when you felt your integrity was the most important value for you.

_____

_____

_____

_____

_____

_____

_____

_____

_____

_____

_____

_____

SELF Defining Questions: INTEGRITY

1)   What tools do I have to support me on the days I feel uninspired?

_____

_____

_____

_____

2)   How much time am I willing to dedicate to finding a way to achieve a more peaceful mind?

_____

_____

_____

_____

3)   How often am I out of integrity with my word to myself and to others?

_____

_____

_____

_____

4)   What is the impact on me and others when I am out of integrity?

_____

_____

_____

_____

_____

_____

_____

5)   What promises to myself and others do I break regularly? What am I willing to do differently in the future? Is there any-where I lie to myself?

_____

_____

_____

_____

_____

Chapter 10

Authenticity

The saying "When one door closes another opens" is true, but only if you are willing to keep your eyes open to actually see another door. That was my experience when I first started my training alliance in 2005. The idea came to mind during a casual conversation with a colleague. I felt as though everything fell into place. In mid-November I decided to start my alliance and by January 4th I was able to launch with a website, brochures and a database of potential clients.

The first year flew by. Sales were good, but not where they needed to be for me to sustain my lifestyle. I was not financially prepared to work for myself with no steady income. My savings were used up quickly and I began incurring debt each month. The second year was much better and I felt very optimistic.

I had experience as a trainer and wanted to add to some personal offerings, so I chose to take several courses to help me expand my skills and to become a certified coach. I used credit to pay for these courses. By the end of year two I could see that I was falling behind. Almost as soon as my credit cards would be full, I'd receive a preapproved card in the mail. I would apply and presto! I had more money available. I have always been optimistic and I thought that any day now the money would start to flow.

Now I know that the line is very fine between being optimistic and having grandiose goals with no financial responsibility.
I didn't tell anyone about my debt. No one would have ever
guessed that I was drowning in it. In the fall of year two I started
to get really scared. I felt the fear in my gut all the time. My sense
of vitality was gone.

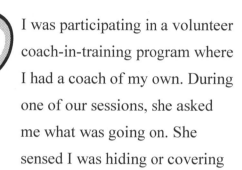

Authenticity
"S"
SELF Expression

I was participating in a volunteer
coach-in-training program where
I had a coach of my own. During
one of our sessions, she asked
me what was going on. She
sensed I was hiding or covering
up something. I didn't answer her because I was petrified of what
might happen if any of the alliance partners found out they had
partnered with someone who was not financially responsible. But
my coach wouldn't let the question go. She asked again. I don't
know what made me spill the beans, but I did. I am still so thankful that she listened and didn't step over what she was present to.
The next day as I was driving home I saw an advertisement
on the side of a bus that said "Debt is Manageable. Call Credit
Canada." I wrote the number down and called when I got home.
The next few weeks were both frightening and a relief at the
same time. I was deeply embarrassed and ashamed, but I told my
children, my parents, my sister, my closest friends and one of the
alliance partners about my debt. Just as I suspected, no one had
a clue that I was in trouble because I always put on a good front.
No one judged me and all offered to help.

My mother came to my rescue several times over the next year to help me keep my vision and business alive.

I worked with a trustee in bankruptcy and we submitted a consumer proposal, which meant that I paid back a portion of my debt over time. I started two part-time jobs to help with cash flow: one as a shoe shine girl two days a week, and a second as a parking attendant on the weekends. I was authentic about and responsible for my finances for the first time in years and it felt liberating. I was very careful over the next year on how I spent both my time and my money. Business picked up and year three was a record year for sales.

Once I took responsibility, told the truth, and said no to continued debt, I could deal with the situation. I have a new respect for money and have put into place structures and support to be certain I stay honest with myself. I recently paid off my consumer proposal and I look forward to a debt-free future.

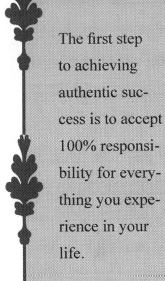

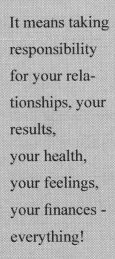

The first step to achieving authentic success is to accept 100% responsibility for everything you experience in your life.

It means taking responsibility for your relationships, your results, your health, your feelings, your finances - everything!

Time to Celebrate!!!

Write about a time when you were truly authentic about some-thing and you felt great about it.

SELF Defining Questions: AUTHENTICITY

1)   What does it mean to me to be truly authentic?

_____

_____

_____

_____

2)   Is this one of my values? If yes why is this important to me?

_____

_____

_____

_____

3)   What lies do I tell myself over and over again? What would change in my life if I stopped lying to myself? What impact could this have on my life?

_____

_____

_____

_____

Live on
Purpose!

Notes

4)   Is there any person or activity that I have to say no to, so I can live a more authentic life?

_____

_____

_____

_____

_____

_____

_____

_____

_____

Chapter 11

Courage

By the time I was 19 years old, I was married with two sons. When people ask me if I loved my first husband, I chuckle. At 17 and pregnant, love didn't really come to mind. Although my first husband and I only lived together until I was expecting my second son, it felt as though we were married.

When I met Dale, I didn't know that he had a criminal record. Ten years earlier, while he was robbing a variety store, he had taken a young boy at gunpoint and told him to run and not look back or he would blow his head off. When he first told me this, he said it really wasn't a big deal because the gun wasn't working and wouldn't have fired anyway. I was flabbergasted because I knew that young boy wouldn't have known that and would have been scared out of his mind.

Still, the first few years of our marriage were pretty good. We had very little money but we got along fairly well. "Fairly well" meant that I did as I was told. Dale worked the night shift and often he'd bring his buddies home for a beer at 7:30 a.m. This always annoyed me because I would be feeding our oldest son, Clinton, when they would come barging into our apartment. One morning, when Clinton was six months old and it was close to Dale's birthday, they all came through the door, laughing, yelling and making all kinds of noise.

I asked them to please be quiet as the baby was sleeping and he wasn't feeling well. Dale told me not to worry, that his kid was tough and could handle it. They turned up the music and started some heavy drinking.

After about an hour Clinton woke up with a fever. I tried to feed him and he didn't want to eat. I gave him some Tempra and laid him back in his crib. As I was coming out of the bedroom I saw one of my husband's buddies put his cigarette butt out on the carpet. I went to Dale and asked him to ask his friends to use the ashtrays. By this time Dale was pretty drunk. Instead of asking his friend to use the ashtray, he grabbed me and pulled my arms behind my back and walked me to the front door and opened the door. I begged him to let me go, that he was hurting me. He said I was nothing but a bitch anyway and threw me out the door.

Courage
"L"
SELF Leadership

I went flying through the doorway and smashed against the wall. Then I heard the door lock. I started to bang on the door and scream for him to let me in. He told me to go to hell and if I wanted to see our baby alive, I would go away and let them have his birthday party. This was in early March; it was still quite cold in Toronto and I was dressed only in a light track suit.

81

I continued to scream and beg him to let me have the baby, that we'd leave them to have their party. The door opened slightly and I thought he was going to let me back in. He didn't. He threw my coat and purse at me and told me to get the hell out of there.

I didn't know what to do. I didn't want to leave and I couldn't stay. I decided to go to my mom and sister's place. I grabbed a cab and when I got to their apartment, I had to call through their mail slot to wake them up. My sister Susan answered the door and was shocked to see me so panicked. I was crying and trying to tell her what had happened. At that point my mom came out of the bedroom, and when she heard what was going on she picked up the phone and called Dale to try to talk some sense into him. It didn't work. He told her to go to hell too.

I sat on the couch, petrified that something would happen to Clinton, my beautiful baby. At that moment, I remembered Dale's criminal record. I told Susan and Mom what I knew and called the police. I told the voice on the other end of the line that my husband was wanted for armed robbery and abduction in Thunder Bay, and that he was keeping my baby from me. The lady on dispatch asked me for the number where I was calling from and told me to stay there until they called me back.

The next hour seemed like an eternity. It was surreal. I felt numb. My sister made coffee and we waited. When the phone rang, I jumped. An officer told me that Dale had been arrested and I could come home.

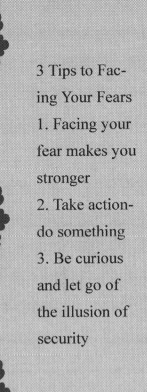

3 Tips to Facing Your Fears
1. Facing your fear makes you stronger
2. Take action- do something
3. Be curious and let go of the illusion of security

I could not have been prepared for what I walked into when I got to my apartment. Everything was torn apart. The contents from the cupboards and dressers were thrown all over the place. At first I thought that the mess was from the party, but the officer explained that because Dale had a charge of armed robbery, they were looking for a gun. When I picked Clinton up out of his crib, I was so relieved that he was fine. From what I could tell, he probably had slept through everything.

After his sentencing, Dale and I did get back together. We had another son, Christopher. For the next three years, things seemed to improve between us. We were a family. Although he both physically and mentally abused me, I thought he was the best man I could get and that I was lucky to have him. I thought this was true because he told me so often how lucky I was that he put up with me, so I began to believe him.

Dale went back to school, obtained his welding license ticket and got a great job. We bought our first home and I enjoyed being a stay-at-home mom. I got to know our neighbours, I helped out at the boys' school, and I become a cub leader. Something inside me was changing: I was feeling more self-confidence. It seemed that the more confident I became, the more possessive Dale became. He started drinking heavily again and often accused me of having an affair. Of course, I was not; I was simply gaining some self-esteem because I was doing things outside the home.

Dale's drinking got so bad that I sometimes had the neighbours help me put him to bed. One day, I said I'd had enough and I decided to leave him. I went to the bank and took out most of our savings, and I went to the apartment building where we used to live. I rented a two-bedroom apartment.

At first I was going to leave without telling him. I planned that one day he would come home from work and the kids and I would be gone. However, I didn't feel right about doing it this way so I told him the week before I was planning move out. He laughed at me and said, "You'll be back."

Dale actually helped us by bringing home some empty boxes. Moving day came and we started settling into our new apartment. I registered the boys in school and looked for a job. Since I had never done anything other than factory work or waitressing, my options were limited. I had to pay the first and last month's rent for the apartment, which left me enough money to live on for about two months. I decided to apply for welfare as a backup plan in case I didn't find work right away. Dale said he would pay support, but I had nothing in writing and I wasn't going to risk that if he didn't help out we would be stranded.

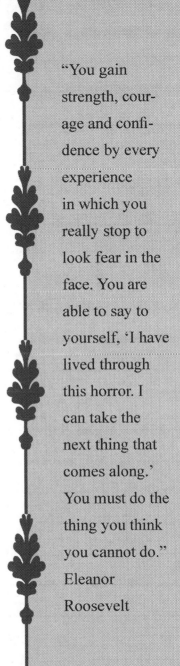

"You gain strength, courage and confidence by every experience in which you really stop to look fear in the face. You are able to say to yourself, 'I have lived through this horror. I can take the next thing that comes along.' You must do the thing you think you cannot do." Eleanor Roosevelt

The kids hated living in an apartment again. They missed their friends and their dad, and they were miserable. Dale called all the time, begging me to come home. I said if we were going to come back, some things needed to change. I agreed to have dinner with him to discuss everything.

During our dinner, Dale made all kinds of promises: not to drink so much, to stop putting me down, to stop accusing me of having an affair, to not hit me anymore and to take me out once in a while to dinner and a movie. So we packed everything up and back the boys and I went. Things were good for about a month until the heavy drinking started again. The difference this time was that I had started to drink as well. One day I was sick from drinking too much, and I knew that our relationship was never going to work. One evening, I was standing at the kitchen sink and something inside of me said, "Get out now!" I did just that.

I did things very differently this time. I consulted a lawyer. We had a legal separation and I moved into a friend's basement so my boys could stay in the neighbourhood and in the same school. Dale's last words to me before I left were, "You haven't got what it takes to make it on your own. You'll be back!" This time he was wrong. My courage propelled me forward.

Time to Celebrate!!!

It's time for some shameless bragging - share about a time when you demonstrated courage to do something. What was it you did? How great did you feel after you were successful? Go ahead BRAG!

_____

_____

_____

_____

_____

_____

_____

_____

_____

_____

Most of what we fear never comes to pass...focus on the positive instead...

Acronym for
FEAR

F – false
E – evidence
A – appearing
R - real

SELF Defining Questions: COURAGE

Questions to ask yourself: 1) What am I afraid of doing?

_____

_____

_____

_____

2)   If I could change anything right now, what would that be?
What's stopping me?

_____

_____

_____

_____

3)   Is there any area of my life where I am settling for what I
have because I lack the courage to change it?

_____

_____

_____

_____

_____

4)   Is there any area of my life where I feel fed up with the way things are? Or am I putting up with something simply because I don't know what to do to change it?

_____

_____

_____

_____

_____

_____

5)   When I read the phrase "Feel the fear and do it anyway," what comes to mind?

_____

_____

_____

_____

_____

Chapter 12

Inspiration

Inspiration is the fuel that has kept me going and that helped me succeed in Toastmasters, an international organization that has helped more than 4 million people around the world become more confident speakers. I'd never thought about participating in a speaking program until after I had an embarrassing presentation. I was working for a manufacturing company and one day I was asked to give an impromptu presentation to the senior leadership team. This was the very first time I had ever stood up in front of a group to present. Although I was nervous when I was waiting for my turn, I was petrified once I stood up. My tongue felt thick, my knees were shaking, and my hands were trembling so badly that a colleague of mine thought I was having a seizure. Though I only spoke for a couple of minutes, it felt like an eternity. Yet I knew everyone in the room and regularly had conversations with them. After the meeting I realized that I had to learn to speak in front of people if I ever wanted a promotion.

About a month later, a colleague and I heard about Toastmasters. We found a club that was close to home for both of us and in the middle of September we went to our first meeting. We were both intimidated by the level of the speakers. We decided that they were way ahead of us and that we should look elsewhere. Neither of us spoke about Toastmasters again until the beginning of the following year, when we decided to go to a meeting and give it another chance. That night we joined and never looked back.

I remember practicing for my icebreaker speech: I threw up before I left my house. When I stood up in front of everyone, I again was terrified. I'd read in the organization's manual that experiencing fear is 100% normal, and that even professionals feel it too. The manual explained that through practice I could learn to control my nervousness and actually learn to embrace it. So I gave my talk anyway.

I've always been a good student, and Toastmasters was no different. I followed the group's recommendations, listened to my mentor and learned from other members. I moved along well until time for my seventh speech.I'd memorized it and I was completely confident that I could deliver a powerful speech. Standing in front of the room, I said my opening and about four sentences, but then I lost my place. Since I'd memorized the speech, I hadn't brought any notes or cue cards. My mind was blank. I stood in silence but nothing came to me. Finally, I sat down, embarrassed.

After the meeting, my mentor came to me and asked me if I was okay. I told her I was upset with my performance and surprised that it happened since I'd memorized my speech. She said that we should never memorize speeches, because if we forget even one small part, we will get stuck.

She shared with me that the most effective way is to remember key points and know your material well, but to not memorize the speech completely. She also said that memorizing only the opening and the closing is a good idea, so that when you are most nervous you will have the opening lines down. By memorizing the closing you can be sure you leave the audience with your intended message.

I grew to love my Toastmaster meetings, not just for the personal growth, but also for the time to be with so many other people who are facing their fears and still getting up and speaking. I never met a Toastmaster I didn't like. I participated in the club executive as the president twice, the VP of public relations, the VP of Membership and the VP of Education. I also served as an Area Governor and ran a Youth Leadership program at a local high school for 20students. I was a member of Toastmasters for over ten years.
I competed and won speech contests, and I have grown beyond what I ever thought possible.

In addition to Toastmasters, I have also attended two training boot camps in the United States. I am driven to improve my ability to engage an audience. My goal is to be an international motivational speaker one day, and I know that through consistent practice I will be on stage in front of thousands of people, inspiring them the way I've been inspired.

Visit a
Toastmasters
Club Near You!
www.toastmasters.org

Notes

Time to Celebrate!!!

Think of a time when you were motivated by pure inspiration to accomplish something. What was the experience like for you?

_____

_____

_____

_____

_____

_____

_____

_____

_____

_____

_____

_____

_____

SELF Defining Questions: INSPIRATION

1)   When was the last time I felt true inspiration?

_____

_____

_____

_____

2)   What was I doing? Is this something I want to experience more in my life?

_____

_____

_____

_____

3)   What difference would it make for myself and others if I were more inspired?

_____

_____

_____

_____

_____

Definition of Inspiration

(Source Dictionary.com)

1. Stimulation or arousal of the mind, feelings, etc, to special or unusual activity or creativity

2. The state or quality of being so stimulated or aroused

3. Someone or something that causes this state

4. An idea or action resulting from such a state

5. The act or process of inhaling; breathing in

94

I've got a
great idea!!!

4)   Who inspires me? What is it about them that inspires me?

_____

_____

_____

_____

_____

_____

5)   What advice would I give to someone who wanted to
know how to live a more inspired life? Am I following my advice in my own life? If not, when would I be willing to start?

_____

_____

_____

_____

_____

_____

_____

Chapter 13

Family

Recently, my oldest son Clinton paid me one of my most cherished compliments. He said that he had never seen such a courageous demonstration of parenting as when I addressed a situation with his younger brother Chris.

As a single mother, I had a few rules that I expected my children to abide by, and one of those was no drugs in our home. To improve my ability to earn income for my family, I was constantly taking night courses, seminars and reading books. When I was 36 I lived with my two teenage boys in a small townhouse in North York. I had known for over a year that I wanted to move into a sales position, and I decided to take a night course to prepare.

One evening I came home early from school because I was not feeling well. As I walked toward the front door I heard loud music from my youngest son's bedroom.
When I walked through the entrance, I smelled marijuana. I ran upstairs, in disbelief, to Chris's room. I didn't knock. I opened the door and caught my son and two of his friends smoking a joint. I yelled and told his friends to leave immediately.

Once they were gone, I asked Chris why he was doing this, knowing my rules. He was angry and protested that marijuana wasn't really a drug. I disagreed. He argued. I told him that often heavy drug users start with marijuana, and I would not tolerate it in my home.

I said he'd have to leave in the morning. He was furious and said I was overreacting. I said no, I had zero tolerance, and Clinton and I wanted to live in a drug-free environment. I told Chris I'd take him somewhere he could figure out what he wanted to do with his life. I didn't sleep all night, tossing, turning, my head spinning with questions. Was I overreacting? What if I let this go? What would be next? I had to preserve our home and he had to realize there were consequences to his actions.

Family
"F"
SELF Motivation

Still, I felt sick. Over breakfast the next morning, I told Chris I was taking him to Seaton House, a men's shelter, where he could think about what he wanted for his future. I told him he could come home if he agreed to the house rules: no drugs, going to school, and getting a part-time job. I felt dead inside when I drove away from the shelter, leaving my youngest son behind. I threw up when I got home.

The next few difficult days were a daze for me, riddled with guilt and uncertainty that I had done the right thing. I was so afraid for him, but at the same time knew that I couldn't expose my other son to the lifestyle his brother was starting to live. My oldest son, Clinton, stayed in touch with Chris initially. Chris was evicted from the shelter because he didn't honour the curfew.

I learned from Clinton that Chris then lived in parks and slept in Goodwill boxes. I was sick with worry.

I'd drive around for hours, hoping to find him and bring him home. Every day, I half-expected to hear that something dreadful had happened to him. I remember many long conversations with my sister, praying that things would work out.

At some point I heard about a tough love group for parents and I went to a meeting. I was very surprised to hear all the horror stories from other parents about their children. Their kids stole cars, committed robbery, dealt and used drugs, and more. I'd felt that Chris's behaviour was partly my fault because I was a single mom and didn't have a male influence for him. After this meeting, I realized that this was not the case. Many of these parents were still married and some were very wealthy. I stopped blaming myself.

After several months of Chris living away from home, I heard that he'd taken a part-time job at a restaurant as a dishwasher. Clinton found out his shift, and I went to the restaurant and waited outside until he came out for his break. He looked surprised to see me waiting for him. Our conversation was a little stiff and uncomfortable at first, but I invited him to come for Sunday dinner the following week. He accepted and I was relieved.

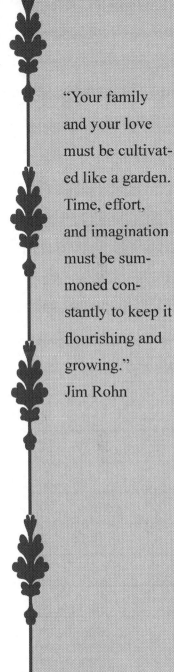

"Your family and your love must be cultivated like a garden. Time, effort, and imagination must be summoned constantly to keep it flourishing and growing."
Jim Rohn

I made all of his favourite foods for dinner, and the event itself that first Sunday was such a comfort. He came for Sunday dinner the next few Sundays as well. One night when he was leaving, he said he'd like to come home. I reminded of the rules and asked if he was ready to abide by them. With a huge grin on his face, he said yes.

I am so proud that Chris stopped doing drugs, completed his education, and is now happily married and is the father of two wonderful children. He is an amazing father, husband and son. He has a brilliant mind and works in computer programming. Chris has said many times that if I hadn't been firm with my family rules, he would have ended up living on the street, the same way some of his other friends did. I am so very fortunate and grateful that things turned out the way they did, and that our family is still together.

Time to Celebrate!!!

Some of my favourite family times were...

_____

_____

_____

_____

_____

_____

_____

_____

_____

_____

_____

_____

_____

_____

"Other things may change us, but we start and end with family"
Anthony Brandt

The saying "If I knew grand-kids were this much fun I would have had them first" is true!!!

SELF Defining Questions: FAMILY

1)   Is family important to me? Why or why not?

_____

_____

_____

_____

2)   Is there anything that I have always wanted to say to anyone in my family that I have been hesitant to say? What would it be like to actually have that conversation? (This could be either a loving conversation or one addressing an issue or conflict.)

_____

_____

_____

_____

3)   What are some of my fondest memories of family? How can I continue to have more experiences like this?

_____

_____

_____

_____

4)   What is my favourite thing to do with my family?

_____

_____

_____

_____

_____

_____

_____

5)   How often do I get together with family? Is this enough for me? If not, how can I create more opportunities to be together?

_____

_____

_____

_____

_____

_____

Chapter 14

Health

Like many people, I've taken my good health for granted. While I had several surgeries in my younger years, I didn't think about my health much through my late thirties. I used to eat what I wanted, I smoked like a chimney, and my fitness plan was irregular. I was fortunate to have a slim build and I didn't have to work at staying that way—at least, not until my fifties.

The only regret I have is that I ever made the choice to start smoking when I was fifteen. I was surrounded by adults who smoked, so to me it was a grown-up thing to do. I asked my dad if I could start smoking, and he said I could, as long as I did it at home and bought my own cigarettes. I learned to smoke in our basement recreation room. I was determined to learn, even though I felt nauseous, dizzy and generally crappy. It took me a little less than a small package of cigarettes to learn to inhale properly without gagging. Of course, this should have been enough to turn me off, but it wasn't. For twenty-three years I smoked, up to two packages a day at times.

I began to think of my cigarettes as my friend and I found comfort in smoking. Sometimes I had very little money for groceries, but I always found a few dollars to buy cigarettes. At that time most of the people I knew smoked and it was acceptable everywhere. I caught colds all the time, and I never connected any of my headaches to cigarettes.

At one time, my mother moved in with me and my two boys. She had quit smoking years earlier. She said when she walked into my room she saw a blue haze of cigarette smoke, and she strongly encouraged me to quit. Once she even paid for me to go to a weekend workshop where I was supposed to learn to quit. A smoker friend of hers joined me for the weekend to support me. He quit for good after that weekend, but I became a closet smoker. I was embarrassed that I had started again so I kept it hidden from my family. At least, I thought I was. My kids knew better. Even though I opened the window in the bathroom and sprayed it with room freshener, my boys could smell the cigarettes. One day I got busted when my oldest son found a cigarette butt with lipstick on it in the toilet that hadn't completely flushed away. I confessed and started to openly smoke again. For the next five years I tried nicotine gum, acupuncture and going cold turkey, but nothing worked. My brother-in-law was convinced that smoking would kill me one day.

Health
"F"
SELF Motivation

I'm not sure how I learned about hypnosis, but I did hear about a doctor that was using hypnosis for quitting smoking. The best part was that because she was a medical doctor, the program was covered by our insurance. I called and put my name on the six-week waiting list. On the day of my first appointment, I smoked like a mad woman beforehand. I wanted to finish every cigarette in my pack before going to the doctor's office.

I waited two hours for my appointment and experienced major withdrawal in the waiting room. I even contemplated leaving to buy a small pack. Finally the nurse called my name and I was relieved that I was finally going to be rid of this addiction forever.

The doctor explained briefly what she would say to me during the session and that I had the free will to stop at any time. She explained that she changes the way a smoker's brain associates with cigarettes. Within a few minutes I was in an altered, calm state. I don't remember what she said while I was under hypnosis, but I walked out of that office and have not smoked since. I returned for the final two sessions because I wanted to make sure I was cured permanently. I still experienced some withdrawal symptoms, but they were very mild compared to what I had felt during the other times I tried to quit.

Smoking is a powerful addiction, and when I started I had no idea of the risks involved. These days, when I see young people smoke I want to pull them aside and urge them to quit, but I know that, like me, they will only quit when they are ready.

I tried to figure out why I was successful at quitting this last time, when I'd failed several times before. I realized that in all the other attempts, I was trying to quit because other people wanted me to. This last time, I wanted to quit smoking for me. I finally placed value on my health and took the steps needed to make it better. It is true when you have your health, you have everything.

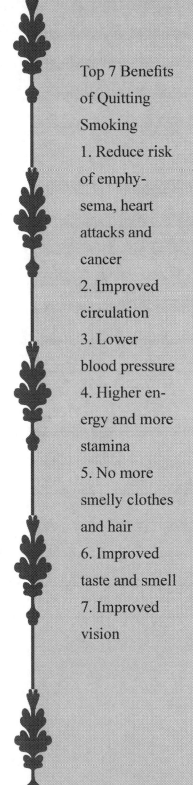

Top 7 Benefits of Quitting Smoking
1. Reduce risk of emphysema, heart attacks and cancer
2. Improved circulation
3. Lower blood pressure
4. Higher energy and more stamina
5. No more smelly clothes and hair
6. Improved taste and smell
7. Improved vision

Notes

Time to Celebrate!!!

Write down some of your best and healthiest habits and behaviours...I am doing so many great things already!

_____

_____

_____

_____

_____

_____

_____

_____

_____

_____

_____

_____

_____

_____

_____

SELF Defining Questions: HEALTH

1)   On a scale from 1 to 10 (with 1 being very sickly and 10 being in optimum health) where would I rate my health? What would it take to move it up one point?

_____

_____

_____

_____

2)   How often do I exercise? Is this enough?

_____

_____

_____

_____

3)   What are some fun ways to exercise?

_____

_____

_____

_____

5 Keys to

Optimum

Health

1.Positive at-

titude

2. Nutrition

3.Exercise

4. Breathing

correctly

5. Regular

cleansing to

remove toxins

4)   Do I smoke, do drugs or drink to excess? Is this something I would like to stop? Do I do anything that I know is not in the best interest of my health? Am I willing to give this up now? How can I commit to this? What am I willing to stop doing to improve my overall health?

_____

_____

_____

_____

_____

_____

_____

_____

5)   What am I willing to start doing to improve my overall health?

_____

_____

_____

Chapter 15

Wonderment

I really do live my life with a sense of wonderment in most areas, in particular in the area of dating. When I left my husband nine years ago, I had no interest in dating and stayed that way for almost two years. Then one day when I was speaking with some ladies at the gym, one of them asked me if I dated much. I laughed and said never! She said she knew a few people who had met their life partners on online dating sites.

At first I dismissed the idea of online dating as too dangerous. Then a few days later, while I was having lunch with a single girlfriend, she shared that she had just set up her profile on an online dating site, and that she was sceptical and excited at the same time. She encouraged me to give it a shot. I went away from lunch wondering, why not?

The next weekend I sat down at my computer and set up my profile. The process was actually quite easy and I selected the one month subscription option. I felt a little tingle of excitement when I received my first email the next morning. I opened the profile of the man who had sent me the email. Talk about a complete let down! I would never go out with someone who looked and sounded like him. Disappointed, I emailed him back and told him I didn't think we were a match and wished him luck.

5 Ideas to help
you live with
more Wonder-
ment

1. Stop,
 Reflect and ask
more "What
If..." questions
2. Play like a
child with no
agenda
3. Network
with other curi-
ous people
4. Be
proactive
5. Put random
ideas together
for possible
creative
 outcomes

Over the next week I averaged four or five emails a day and I had the same reaction to them all. I didn't wait until my month was up to delete my profile. I was convinced that online dating wasn't for me. Yet over the next several months, I heard about more and more people who were meeting wonderful partners on various online dating sites. I wondered if maybe I'd given up too soon. I wasn't meeting potential men at any of the other events I was participating in, so I wondered if I should try again. That is what I did. Only the second time, I approached it with a more optimistic attitude. I decided I was going to have some fun.

Wonderment
"E"
SELF Esteem

As I uploaded my pictures this time, I decided to include a few shots of me having fun and laughing, instead of my business picture that I used on the first site. I also kept the "in my own words" section of my profile light and easy.

I couldn't help but notice the difference in the men that contacted me after I changed my attitude. I began to really enjoy the back and forth banter, and meeting for coffees, drinks, dinner, dancing and walks in the park. I realized I was starting to have a social life. Now I was not as disappointed when the men I was meeting were not a fit: instead, I took the attitude that meeting the right man was just a matter of time. While I had many dates over the years thanks to online dating, none have made me as excited as the one that I am going on tonight. It seems appropriate to write this section today, while I'm feeling butterflies and more excitement than I have felt in years. I'm meeting a gentleman that contacted me a week ago. When I first saw his picture, I thought, "WOW, this guy looks really good!" I read his profile: 57 years old, 6 feet tall and lived not too far from me. We exchanged a few emails, and it was apparent he was intelligent and interesting (a rare combination online!). We chatted on the phone, and as crazy as it sounds, I felt a connection with him. After I got off the phone, I found myself smiling and I was very excited to meet him.

The next morning I received an email from him, saying how much he enjoyed our conversation and that he was looking forward to meeting me. We've been in communication every day since. For me this is a new experience; most of the time when people meet someone online and they set a time to meet, they don't communicate.

I woke up this morning feeling like a school girl again. This is true wonderment in action! I received an email from him at 8:06 am, saying only 11 hours to go.... My stomach flipped. I wonder, could he be the one for me?

Now, writing this later, I must tell you that we had a great time on our date, but I could see during the following week that we were not a fit. I am still searching for a loving relationship, and I wonder, when I will meet the right man? Living with wonderment about everything, including dating, helps me keep my life light and my curiosity alive.

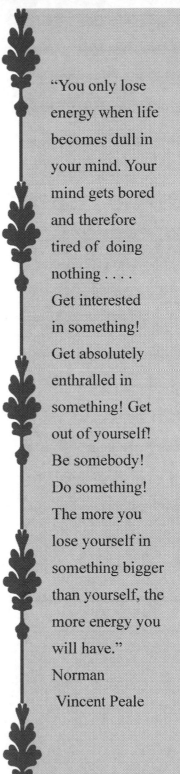

"You only lose energy when life becomes dull in your mind. Your mind gets bored and therefore tired of doing nothing . . . . Get interested in something! Get absolutely enthralled in something! Get out of yourself! Be somebody! Do something! The more you lose yourself in something bigger than yourself, the more energy you will have."
Norman Vincent Peale

Notes

Time to Celebrate!!!

When was the last time you were amazed by something? What was it?

_____

_____

_____

_____

_____

_____

_____

_____

_____

_____

_____

_____

_____

SELF Defining Questions: WONDERMENT

1)   What does wonderment mean to me?

_____

_____

_____

_____

2)   Are there any areas in my life where I have become re-signed about life? What would bringing a little more curiosity to my life do?

_____

_____

_____

_____

3)   What really gets me excited and feeling like a schoolchild again? How can I bring more of this into my life?

_____

_____

_____

_____

I'm curious...

What?

How?

Why?

When?

Why not?

4)   Is it important for me to keep some of my childlike curiosity? What difference can this make?

_____

_____

_____

_____

_____

_____

_____

_____

_____

_____

Chapter 16

Friendship

I have been blessed with many friends over the years. I love the saying that people come into our lives for a reason, a season or a lifetime. This perspective has allowed me to understand why some people come in to challenge us and help us grow, while others come to nurture us and to be the shoulder to cry on when we need it. It also has provided me with the understanding that when people move on, that our purpose together has been fulfilled. I know people that have maintained friendships from their childhood. I haven't had that experience, because I moved away from the small town where I grew up and I didn't stay in touch with anyone. People have come into and gone from my life, and I have laughed, cried and had many different experiences with them.

I have learned a lot from my friends, mostly what it takes to be a friend. For many years I thought the way to be a friend was to be nice and agree with everyone, don't rock any boats and make sure things stay status quo. I no longer believe that this is what friends do for each other. True friendship is the same as any other relationship: there are ups and downs. The biggest mistake we can make is to ignore things. I have done this often over the years, and last year I realized that, in the end, this can erode a friendship. If we hold things inside, eventually they will come out. Often that will be in a situation where emotions are high, and sometimes we say things that hurt the very people we care so much about. One of my dearest friends for the past eight years used to be late for everything we planned. I, on the other hand, am usually a little early or right on time. We'd make plans to go out for an evening and we'd decide on a central place to meet so we could go in one car. Time and again I'd wait in a parking lot for twenty to thirty minutes. As each minute went by I'd become more and more upset. When my friend would finally arrive, I'd be so relieved to be on our way that I wouldn't

Friendship "E" SELF Esteem

say anything. I didn't want to upset her, especially since we were going to spend the evening together. This happened more times than I can count, until I found myself avoiding making plans with her.

One day while we were chatting on the phone, she commented that we hadn't been out in a long time. I felt the need to tell her the truth. I told her how upset it made me that she was always late, that I was afraid of losing the friendship and upsetting her, so I hadn't said anything before. She said she knew it wasn't right for her to be always late, but she never realized how much it bothered me because I never told her. I confessed that I was actually avoiding her because it was too upsetting to me to be left in parking lots anymore. She laughed and asked why I didn't just come later if I knew she was going to be late. I said that would be out of character for me as I do everything within my power to be where I say I'm going to be when I say I'll be there. I could see then that I'd created this mess by not speaking up sooner. We've agreed that if either of us is going to be more than five minutes late, we'll call each other. The most beautiful part of this situation is that it has deepened our relationship and we now have more open communication. The bonus is that, now, most of the time she is either right on time or even a little early.

Sometimes we fear the worst will happen when we speak up, but often the outcome is the exact opposite. I met a lady at a singles' function about 7 years ago. I had joined this group so that I could make some single friends. On the way to Niagara for a wine tour with the group, I sat beside this lady. We chatted and hit it off right away, and we even exchanged phone numbers and said we would go dancing together. A few weeks later we connected and decided to go to one of the singles' dances. She didn't drive, so I offered to pick her up. We had a lot of fun and said we'd do it again soon.

Over the next few months we went out a few more times and got to know more about each other. This friend was quite different than me when it came to ambition: she seemed content with her life, while I was always taking a seminar, reading a new book and creating new opportunities in my life. Often she'd ask me when I was going to be satisfied. I asked her what she meant, and she said that I was always setting new goals and learning new things, and she wondered when I was going to settle down.

I was quite disturbed by her interpretation of what I was doing with my life. I explained that I wanted to start my own business, and become an author and a keynote speaker. I could see from her look that she felt I was wasting my time.

9 Tips on Being a Great Friend
1. Celebrate her success
2. Be Honest
3. Share secrets & keep them secrets
4. Be grateful
5. Use your manners (say please and thank you)
6. Be there in good times and bad
7. Accept her for who she is
8. Give and take
9. Let go of toxic relationships

Honesty
is the best
policy...
everytime!!!

After that I was very careful in what I shared with her. One day she called and, hearing the excitement in my voice, asked what was going on. I told her that I had a great training opportunity and I was preparing the presentation. I cut the call short and went back to working on my presentation. Unfortunately, I never got the opportunity to present my proposal because my potential client announced they were merging with another organization and would not be doing any external training, which was disappointing. When my friend asked how my presentation went, I told her that it had been cancelled. She said that it was so like me to set my sights too high and then be disappointed, and she didn't understand why I did it.

After that incident I felt she was not on my side at all. I questioned whether we were actually contributing to each other's lives. The answer was no. I called her and said that we had very different views on life and I didn't think we had much in common. I explained that rather than just avoiding her and pretending to be too busy to get together, that I preferred to tell her the truth. She sounded a little upset at first, but once we talked it through, she agreed that we really didn't share many of the same values or philosophies. After there was no expectation to continue the friendship, I realized that I felt lighter, and I freed up time to do more things that were in alignment with my goals. Occasionally I see her at events and we still chat. There are no hard feelings. I made a promise going forward to respect my values in all my relationships, and to have those difficult conversations when necessary. In this way I will honour my friends as well as myself.

Time to Celebrate!!!

Think of a time when your friendship made a difference for someone.

_____

_____

_____

_____

_____

_____

_____

_____

_____

_____

_____

_____

_____

_____

SELF Defining Questions: FRIENDSHIP

1)   What does friendship mean to me? How does having friends impact my life?

_____

_____

_____

_____

2)   Are there friends that are less than supportive of me? Maybe they put me down or say my ideas are dumb. If yes, do they still bring value to my life in other ways?

_____

_____

_____

_____

3)   How would people describe me as a friend? Would I want to be my own friend?

_____

_____

_____

_____

4)   What are some of the things I like doing with my friends? How can I do more of these things?

_____

_____

_____

_____

_____

_____

_____

_____

5)   Do I have the skills to have difficult conversations with friends when things come up? Do I think it is important to have the same shared values as my friends? Why or why not?

_____

_____

_____

_____

_____

Definition of Friend
(Source: Dictionary.com)

1. A person known well to another and regarded with liking, affection, and loyalty; an intimate

2. An acquaintance or associate

3. An ally in a fight or cause; supporter

4. A fellow member of a party, society, etc

5. A patron or supporter

Conclusion

I hope you have enjoyed my stories and have learned something new about yourself by answering the SELF defining questions. I have grown a lot over the years and through one choice at a time I have become more SELF defined. We cannot always choose the events that happen in our lives but we can choose our responses to these events. I have learned this first hand from the many varied experiences in my life.

I live by my values and make choices every day that align with who I have become. I encourage you to write your own book and provide others the opportunity to learn from your life experiences too!

In Love and Gratitude

Cindy

www.awomansjourney.ca